Items should be returned on or before the last date
shown below. Items not already requested by other
borrowers may be renewed in person, in writing or by
telephone. To renew, please quote the number on the
barcode label. To renew online a PIN is required.
This can be requested at your local library.
Renew online @ **www.dublincitypubliclibraries.ie**
Fines charged for overdue items will include postage
incurred in recovery. Damage to or loss of items will
be charged to the borrower.

Leabharlanna Poiblí Chathair Bhaile Átha Cliath
Dublin City Public Libraries

Dublin City
Baile Átha Cliath

D1579570

Date Due	Date Due	Date Due
0 3 JUN 2010		

Contents

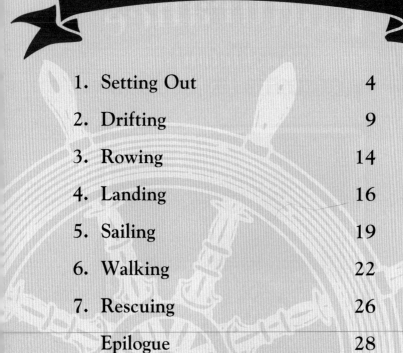

Twenty-eight men stood in the middle of a frozen ocean and watched as their ship sank beneath the ice. Their last link with home, comfort, and normal life was gone. All around them, there was nothing but ice. There was no inhabited land for hundreds of kilometres. The temperature was way below freezing, day and night. They were completely alone.

This was the beginning of one of the most incredible stories of survival in human history.

1. Setting Out

Sir Ernest Shackleton's Imperial Trans-Antarctic Expedition left England in August 1914. His goal was to cross Antarctica from sea to sea via the South Pole. This had never been done before.

Shackleton planned every detail carefully. They would sail to Antarctica in the beautiful new sail-and steam-powered ship *Endurance*, which was especially designed for breaking through sea ice. Then they would walk the 2400 kilometres across the continent, using dog sleds to carry their supplies.

They would take films and photographs and make scientific observations along the way. Another ship was to meet them at the other end of the journey to take them home. As it happened, things didn't work out that way.

The route of the *Endurance* from England to South Georgia

The intended route of the Imperial Trans-Antarctic Expedition from South Georgia to the Ross Sea

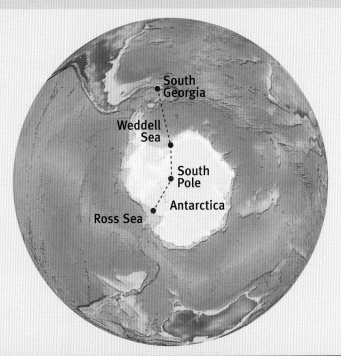

On 5 November 1914, the *Endurance* reached the island of South Georgia, the departure point for Antarctica. On board were twenty-eight men and sixty-nine sled dogs. Frank Worsley, the ship's captain, and Frank Hurley, the photographer, climbed a high peak on the island and were impressed by the jagged, hurricane-battered ranges. Worsley observed in his diary:

I heard that no one had ever crossed the island.

He would not have dreamed that eighteen months later he would cross these mountains himself.

The South Georgia whalers told Shackleton that the Antarctic **pack ice** was further north that year than anyone could remember. He waited a month for the ice to clear, but it didn't. The men were eager to get going. Shackleton decided not to wait any longer. The *Endurance* set sail, and the expedition was under way.

Just three days later, they came to the first of the pack ice. Shackleton ordered the captain to press on. The men's spirits were high. They enjoyed crashing through the ice in the ship. They sang to the penguins on the **ice floes** with their banjo and bagpipes.

Further and further into the icy Weddell Sea they sailed, and on 19 January 1915, they finally sighted the Antarctic coast, only 50 kilometres away. Two more hours' steaming through open water and they would be there.

But there was no open water. The pack ice closed around the *Endurance*, and it was stuck.

The trapped ship drifted north with the ice, back the way it had come. The men watched helplessly as the land they had almost reached became more and more distant and then disappeared.

2. Drifting

For nine months, the *Endurance* drifted. The explorers prepared to face the long Antarctic winter, where the sun doesn't rise for ninety days. They thought that if they could just survive until the spring when the ice melted, they would be able to carry on.

Instead, the melting of the ice was the ship's downfall. As the ice thinned, it cracked, releasing the ship back into the water but trapping it between grinding ice floes.

Early in August, the men heard noises like guns going off. The ship's timbers were breaking as the ice floes squeezed it, forcing it up and out onto its side. For the *Endurance*, it was the beginning of the end.

The ship shrieks and quivers, windows splinter, while the deck timbers gape and twist.

Frank Hurley's diary, 26 October 1915

Finally, at the end of October, Shackleton and his men abandoned ship. They took the three lifeboats, tents, tools, and as much food as they could and camped on a solid floe.

Ship too dangerous to live in.
We are forced to abandon her.

Frank Worsley's diary, 27 October 1915

The broken *Endurance* finally sank on 21 November. Shackleton felt the loss deeply, but he immediately started planning how they could reach land and safety.

A man must shape himself to a new mark
directly the old one goes to ground.

Shackleton, in his book *South*

For five months, the men lived on the ice in five small tents. They hunted seals and penguins for food. They used seal **blubber** for fuel and lighting. They melted ice for drinking water.

Camping on a drifting ice floe was uncomfortable and dangerous. The men were always wet and cold. If they warmed up, they got wetter. If they got colder, their clothes froze. Sometimes a man fell through a crack in the ice and had to be hauled up. Everyone feared that the floe might split underneath them as they slept. Unstoppable icebergs ploughed through the pack ice, narrowly missing them. Killer whales often surrounded the floe, hoping for a change of diet from seals.

**Shackleton and Hurley
preparing a meal**

Passing time on the ice

Shackleton's party spent 15 months on the ice, at first in the stranded ship, and then camped on an ice floe. The men helped pass the time by:

- training and racing the dog teams
- playing football
- reading the books they had brought with them, including the *Encyclopedia Britannica*
- singing songs, accompanied by Leonard Hussey's banjo
- playing cards
- reciting any poems they could remember
- telling stories
- talking about their travels
- discussing the weather (was the wind blowing their floe north?)
- describing their favourite meals in great detail – endlessly.

The ship's captain, Frank Worsley, even went swimming once!

The men's only hope now rested in the three small lifeboats saved from the *Endurance*. They knew that when their floe melted, they would have to launch the boats into the sea. It was a prospect they dreaded.

Twice, they attempted to walk to land across the ice. But the boats were too heavy to pull very far, and they did not dare leave them behind.

It was a sad day when the men finally agreed that they had to destroy the sled dogs, who had been their companions and entertainers for so long. They needed too much food, and there would be no room for them in the boats when the ice melted.

3. Rowing

On 9 April, 163 days after the men set up camp on the drifting floe, the watchman raised the alarm that the ice was splitting. Several times, the men had to move all their gear to avoid the cracks, and to keep everyone on the same piece of the floe. Finally, they had to hurriedly pack everything they could into their three boats and cast off into the rough, freezing sea. They rowed as fast as they could to get away from the shattering ice.

They were now in the most dangerous part of the Southern Ocean, where huge waves met the churning ice floes. They had no water to drink at all. The men's lips and tongues became so swollen they could hardly swallow. Everyone was sick and frostbitten.

After seven terrible days and nights, they reached the barren rock of Elephant Island – the first people ever to land there.

Landing on Elephant Island

The men left behind on Elephant Island

4. Landing

While Shackleton (who hadn't slept for four days) organised hot drinks, the men reeled around, running their hands through the pebbles on the beach. They were on land – solid, unmoving land – the first they had been on since leaving South Georgia. Their cracked lips bled as they laughed with joy and relief.

They had enough food left for just five weeks. Shackleton realised that they had no hope of being rescued from Elephant Island, so he set about planning the next step: a journey in one of the boats to get help.

The only inhabited place they had the remotest chance of reaching was South Georgia, 1300 kilometres away. One of the lifeboats, the *James Caird*, was prepared for the seemingly impossible journey. This little boat was to take on the huge waves and gales of the Southern Ocean. It was their only hope.

Shackleton selected five of the toughest men to make the journey with him: Worsley, Crean, McNeish, McCarthy, and Vincent. Just before they set out, Shackleton confessed to Worsley that he had no experience in small-boat sailing. Worsley replied, "All right, boss. I do."

The *James Caird*

The *James Caird* was about 7 metres long and 2 metres across. McNeish, the carpenter, created a flimsy covering over the front of the boat to provide some protection for the men from the full force of waves and spray. The decking was made of box lids and sled runners. Pieces of torn canvas were sewn together (with bleeding and frostbitten fingers) and nailed to this decking. To make the boat watertight, its seams were **caulked** with **lamp wick** and the expedition artist's oil paints, then finished off with seal blood.

The boat was loaded with:

- **ballast** – more than a tonne of shingle and stones in bags made from blankets
- sleeping bags
- food for 30 days
- a **Primus** stove and oil lamp
- drinking water
- navigation equipment.

Hurley's photographs, Worsley's **log**, and Shackleton's diary were also stowed in the boat.

5. Sailing

On Easter Monday, 1916, the *James Caird* cast off from Elephant Island into the roughest ocean in the world. The men who were left behind built a shelter under the two remaining lifeboats and prepared for a long, cold wait.

For the men on the sea, it was a nightmare journey. They had only a tiny space to sleep in on top of the stores and ballast. Every time a wave hit, everyone was flung around. Two sleeping bags became so wet they were useless – that left four bags between six men. It was so cold that one night Worsley couldn't straighten his body out after a spell at the **tiller**. He had to be massaged until he could unfold himself enough to get into his bag.

Frank Worsley, the navigator, had to get the *James Caird*'s course exactly right. If the boat missed South Georgia, it would sail on into the empty south Atlantic Ocean, blown by the westerly gales, and all twenty-eight men would face certain death. Worsley's main tool was the sextant, an instrument that uses the sun and stars to determine position.

In seventeen days, Worsley managed only four sun sightings. Two men had to prop him up when he was taking readings, so that he didn't fall overboard. At night, he steered by the feel of the wind.

The men wouldn't have survived the cold and wet without hot food. They cooked below, on a Primus stove. One man held the lamp, and two men balanced the Primus between their feet, bracing their backs against the boat's sides. Meals consisted of "hoosh" – dried beef protein, lard, porridge, sugar, and salt. They boiled this up every four hours. At night, they made a hot drink every four hours.

By the fifth day, the **hull** was covered in ice, putting the boat in danger of sinking. The men had to climb onto the frozen canvas to hack off the ice while the boat was rolling.

When they opened the last cask of water, they found it was salty because of a leak. It was the only water they had, so they had to drink it, about a cup a day.

At last they saw land, through thick fog. A fierce hurricane blew them into the coast, and the boat was in danger of being hurled onto rocks. They finally found a narrow gap in the reef, and with great skill brought the boat through.

It was 10 May 1916. The six men had survived sixteen days and nights in a tiny boat in the wild Southern Ocean, navigating 1300 kilometres to reach their goal against all the odds. But their boat was broken and could not sail the 250 kilometres around the island to Stromness whaling station for help.

They were so near to safety – and yet so far from it. Standing between the whaling station and the six forlorn, half-dead men was that range of unmapped, unclimbed mountains that Worsley and Hurley had seen at the start of the expedition.

6. Walking

Shackleton knew that the mountains of South Georgia were considered too difficult for even strong, well-equipped climbers to cross. But he was not a man to give up, especially since the lives of the twenty-two men on Elephant Island also depended on his rescue party.

The three fittest men, Shackleton, Worsley, and Crean, prepared to attempt the crossing. They were sailors, with no mountaineering skills. They were by now physically weak. Their boots were falling apart, but McNeish patched them with screws from the boat for grip on the ice. Their clothes were worn out.

They decided not to carry sleeping bags but to walk night and day. They took an axe, some rope, a lamp, the Primus, logbooks, compasses, and food for three days. They knew they could survive no longer than that.

The three men set out at 2 a.m. on May 19. By four in the afternoon, they were high on a ridge and fog was rolling in. They knew that if they didn't get down, they would freeze to death overnight.

There was no path, only very steep slopes. So they sat down one behind the other, linked up, and slid down into the darkness. They covered 300 metres in three minutes. Worsley recorded in his diary:

We seemed to shoot into space. For a moment my hair stood on end. Then quite suddenly I felt a glow and knew that I was grinning. I was actually enjoying it. It was most exhilarating. We were shooting down the side of an almost precipitous mountain at nearly a mile a minute!

They walked on in pitch darkness until the moon rose, lighting their way. They had a meal and plodded on. At 5 a.m., they rested, arms around each other. Right away, Worsley and Crean fell into a deep sleep. Shackleton knew they would die of cold if he didn't wake them. He shook them awake after five minutes, told them they'd slept for half an hour, and they all went on.

At half past six, they heard the morning siren from the whaling station far below. "Never had any of us heard sweeter music," Shackleton later recalled.

They came to a waterfall in their way. They flung the axe, the logbooks, and the Primus down before them, then tied their rope to a boulder. Worsley and Shackleton lowered Crean, the heaviest man, first; Shackleton went next, then Worsley. They left the rope there.

They were shivering, soaking wet, and freezing, but elated. The whaling station was only two kilometres away.

Two boys were the first people to see the men. The boys ran away, terrified by these scary figures with long beards and matted hair, wearing filthy clothes, by now ripped to shreds – clothes they hadn't changed for nearly a year.

The men found the manager of the whaling station. He was astonished to see them, and asked who they were. He didn't recognise them as the explorers he'd farewelled eighteen months earlier.

"My name is Shackleton," said the wild man.

Their welcome then was tremendous. While the three exhausted men recovered, the whalers sailed around to pick up the other three men, and the heroic little boat, from the other side of the island. Then Shackleton set about planning the final task – the rescue of the twenty-two men waiting on Elephant Island.

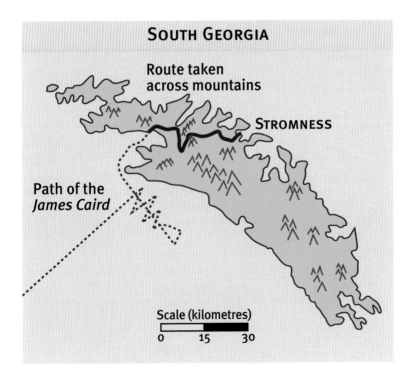

SOUTH GEORGIA

Route taken across mountains

STROMNESS

Path of the *James Caird*

Scale (kilometres)

0   15   30

7. Rescuing

Shackleton tried four times to rescue the rest of the men. Three times, he was defeated by the ice. By August, it looked as though the men would have to stay on Elephant Island until the summer – if they could survive that long.

In a last desperate attempt, Shackleton borrowed an old steel trawler, the *Yelcho*, from the Chilean government. Just as it arrived at Elephant Island on 30 August 1916, a wide path opened through the pack ice, and the *Yelcho* slipped through.

The marooned men had almost given up hope. It was the painter, George Marston, and the photographer, Frank Hurley, who first noticed the little ship steaming around an iceberg. The others did not believe it at first. Then, Hurley recalled, when they realised that help had at last arrived, "they came crawling through the roof and breaking through the walls, frantic with joy".

When Shackleton was within calling distance, he yelled, "Are you all well?"

"We are all well, boss," came Frank Wild's reply.

Everyone was safe on the trawler within an hour, as the ice began to close in again. There was no time for the castaways to show their rescuers the camp they had built underneath the two upturned lifeboats. All they took from the island were the precious photographic **plates** and reels of film. They watched their home of the last five months recede as they stood on the deck, munching the apples and oranges that Shackleton had brought for them. The fruit tasted incredibly delicious.

Epilogue

Every member of the Imperial Trans-Antarctic Expedition lived to tell the tale. Their amazing survival was largely due to the men's good humour, resourcefulness, and co-operative spirit. They also owed much to the seamanship and navigational skill of Frank Worsley.

But above all, their survival was due to the leadership of Sir Ernest Shackleton, whose courage, determination, and faith provided the example and inspiration they needed to endure the almost unendurable.

Records of the journey

Photographs and film

Frank Hurley kept his boxes of photographic plates and movie film in sealed containers. They spent two weeks under mushy ice in the wreck of the *Endurance* before they were salvaged, and then almost a year buried under snowdrifts at the ice camp and on Elephant Island. When they were finally processed, they revealed images of great beauty and drama.

Paintings

George Marston, the expedition's artist, painted many scenes of the adventure.

Journals, logs, and books

Several men kept journals, including Hurley, Worsley, and Shackleton, who all wrote books about the adventure afterwards.

1914	August	*Endurance* leaves England
	November 5	*Endurance* arrives at South Georgia
	December 5	Expedition departs for Antarctica
1915	January 19	Ship beset by ice – drifting north
	August 1	Ship begins to break up
	October 27	Men abandon ship – set up camp on ice
	November 21	*Endurance* sinks
1916	April 9	Men take to lifeboats when floe breaks up
	April 16	Boats land on Elephant Island
	April 24	*James Caird* leaves Elephant Island with 6 men
	May 10	*James Caird* lands at South Georgia
	May 19	3 men set out to cross the mountains
	May 20	Men reach Stromness; other 3 rescued
	August 30	Last 22 men rescued from Elephant Island

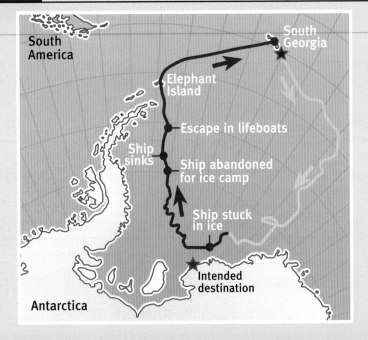

Glossary

(These words are printed in bold type
the first time they appear in the book.)

ballast: heavy material carried on a boat to help keep it steady

blubber: the fat of marine mammals such as seals and sea lions

caulk: to fill in the gaps in a boat's sides with waterproof material

hull: the basic shell of a boat

ice floe: a sheet of floating sea ice

lamp wick: the woven cord that carries the fuel to the flame in an oil lamp

log: the daily record of a journey or expedition

pack ice: a large area of ice floes packed together by wind and currents

plates: sheets of specially treated glass that old cameras used to capture images

Primus: the brand name of a type of portable oil stove

tiller: the lever that turns a boat's rudder to steer it

Index